LOOKI[N] GH[OST]

SEEKER OF TRUTH

Written by

Thomas Andrew Warrington

This book is dedicated to and also written in loving memory of *Colin Warrington*

You were an inspiration to me and everybody around you.

A truly magnificent person who had a definitive abundance of love and compassion for his family and friends.

We shall never forget you.

-

Grandad

CONTENTS

About the author

-

Chapter 1 – *The Humming Lady of Aby*

Chapter 2 – *The Ghostly Scenario*

Chapter 3 – *The Ruskington Horror*

Chapter 4 – *Ghosts, UFOS and the Almighty Lord*

Chapter 5 – *Paranormal Wars*

Chapter 6 – *Spirited Pubs and Inns*

Chapter 7 – *Haverholme Priory*

Chapter 8 – *The Erratic Nature of the Modern Day Ghost Hunter*

Chapter 9 – *Seeking the Truth*

-

Acknowledgements

Appendix:

Recommended reading to further the curiosity into the unknown

About the Author

I was born on the 17th September 1984 in Boston Pilgrim Hospital, located east of rural Lincolnshire (possibly the best decade of all time, but not for the fashion I must add).

Brought up in a small rural village in Heckington for the majority of my life, it was here that I spent most of my childhood. This mostly consisted of frantic den building in fields with friends with the main aim being to achieve an impressive structure allowing us to laugh, share our dreams (and more importantly) to bond in a way that children should. Shielded from the craziness of the outside world, the dens were built mainly of carefully constructed wood gathered from nearby.

As a boy I always had a thought in the back of my mind, that the world could be a dangerous and scary place, consisting of emotional curve balls and intersections of decisions that could change your destiny forever. But being around friends those thoughts never materialised, instead, only care and compassion were present amongst the group.

In life we go through good times and bad, but I believe that every negative can be utilised into a positive motion. If life was a tapestry then one could say that the bad times are simply dropped stitches, of which in time can be re-sown.

On Halloween 1992, an infamous show aired for the first time on the BBC. I can still to this day remember having my small TV placed precariously on the edge of my white desk (covered in stickers varying from wrestlers to Teenage Mutant Ninja Turtles) this would be the setting of a monumental night for me, and has left its mark to this very day. Now as mentioned, instances and decision making can change your path in life and this decision certainly did that for me.

"Ghost Watch" was a live TV broadcast presented similarly to Crimewatch, which gave it a very clinical approach. The writer behind the show was a man called Stephen Volk who remarkably, was interviewed by me 28 years after the original broadcast was aired on the BBC. The show was filmed live and the viewers were duped into thinking that the presenters and the film crew were investigating claims of supernatural happenings in a typical family home in England.

The show (following on from the live broadcast) later announced that it was all fabricated, but nevertheless it scared The Nation including a young Thomas Warrington.

The ghost/entity was predominately moulded on the Enfield haunting, with very similar types of phenomena taking place in the family's home. It certainly terrified me and (much to the annoyance of my mum and Dad) I resided in their room for many weeks after viewing this dramatic and horrifying staged haunting. Who knows, if I had watched something else that night maybe my passion would have never of materialised?

The interest in ghosts certainly stemmed from watching the show, but I then received a book on my 10th birthday, which was a Strange but True casebook of the Enfield poltergeist. Given as a gift from my Uncle Mark Steadman, this was certainly to further galvanise what started as an interest and has now projected a lifelong search for the truth, whilst trying to gauge an understating of what people claim to experience…

Turning the clocks forward, I now live in Sleaford, Lincolnshire with my wife Gemma and my two children Charlie and Chanelle … not forgetting my ghost detector Jahrah the dog.

Over the years I have been involved with paranormal groups and individuals from various locations across the UK. This has demonstrated many different methods and practices. And also (having been involved at the start with a small group from Spalding) it certainly did open up a whole new world and gave my interest a further push into the realm of the unknown.

Going further on in time, I then helped create a group that was based in Nottinghamshire. We prided ourselves on discovering locations and abodes that had never been investigated before.

At this point in my life the group had achieved some amazing feats and investigated some very peculiar places, ranging from caves in Mansfield to the Stonebow arch in the city of Lincoln. Certainly the most memorable moment was planning and conducting a public ghost hunt at the beautiful Stonebow Guildhall. This was by no means a normal evening, as not only was we the only team to have done anything like this at this stunning location, but in attendance was the Mayor of Lincoln himself and supported by all his dignitaries…. (a very peculiar night indeed, but certainly a night I will never forget).

A couple of years passed with the group from Nottinghamshire, and I felt that it was time to take a different path and approach to paranormal investigating. I am truly thankful for the experiences and time attained with these groups, as it has given me an advantage and better understanding of the public and events aspect of the paranormal realm. Further to this it also allowed me to observe how others conduct themselves within a public paranormal event.

I soon found myself getting the writing bug as I was witnessing some very frustrating notions within public events and felt I needed to swiftly put pen to paper. I have written many articles for magazines in the UK covering many angles within the paranormal, but mainly on the subject of ghosts and hauntings.

It's been many years now since I was part of a group/team that conduct themselves in a collective way, but I don't think I could ever imagine re-visiting this popular way of involvement with the subject matter.

My time within groups has passed and I do believe that you need to find what works best for you. I have found that being a lone investigator is certainly much more beneficial for me.

In 2015 I was approached to appear on some radio shows to talk about my interest, and ideology with regards to what a haunting could be...... As we are all aware, the secret of unlocking the answers to the paranormal seems to be still of a distant goal, and I do wonder whether we are destined to know the secrets of the mind and also the universe itself.

Following a series of online interviews and talks with local newspapers, I was contacted by Carl Warr from Pulse Talk Radio (an online radio station based on the Isle of white) and asked to present my own weekly show incorporating all areas under the paranormal umbrella. I was very taken aback by the approach and at the same time extremely grateful for the offer from Carl.

The invitation was gladly accepted in November 2016 and "The Pure Paranormal Show" was born and is still currently being broadcast today. It would be a lie if I didn't say how proud I am of having created the show, but all thanks to Carl Warr for initially giving me the opportunity.

The show will be 4 years old this November 2020 and we have had some incredible guests from around the world, each bringing their knowledge and expertise to tantalise and mystify the listener.

The very first episode of the show aired on the dark and chilly evening of 22nd November 2016. I can recall how petrified I was prior to going live, but I had prepared layouts and questions which certainly ensured it wasn't a complete disaster right from kick off. Now I must mention the very first guest on the show, as to this day we have stayed in touch, and she has recently appeared on a birthday edition of the show.

"The Reluctant Ghost Hunter" AKA the lovely Joanna Cowell, was my first victim/guest on an adventure that hasn't stopped and has created new bonds and friendships with people from all walks of life, which is so important to me.

A heartfelt thank you to Joanna, as she made it a lot easier for me to conduct the interview and I managed to start breathing properly approximately half way through the show. I have so much love and affection for the show as it has enabled me to build new relations, and has allowed me to engage with listeners/groups and individuals from around the globe.

In an unusually warm March of 2017, I stumbled across a chap named Barry Frankish online. He caught my eye with his ideology and general persona, which in some ways I saw as a reflection of myself. He agreed to be interviewed for episode 13 aired on the 7th of March 2017. The interview was a great success and a bond was quite profoundly instantaneous, and you could say the rest was history as of that very first discussion. Barry was featured on a number of episodes and I soon realised that we had a double act of fused calmness and plenty of theories for people to debate on. Barry was then asked to be the co-host of the show from the summer of 2017 and I felt we had found the partnership the show required.

He is another really important person that I am very thankful I crossed paths with, and without him researching and conducting the show would definitely be more stressful and certainly a lot more chaotic.

What does the future hold for me? Well I will certainly hope to be doing more lectures at conventions and also to continue writing articles regarding the paranormal. I would like to thank everyone who has engaged with me this far in my life… I am a big believer that things happen for a reason and it is how we tackle issues and embrace life for what it is in our journey to fulfil our life expectations….

I would also like to thank the people that nearly caused me to walk away from the paranormal field indefinitely. Your negativity and blindness has spurred me on to achieve some amazing accomplishments, and as stated earlier, I believe you can turn negative energy into a more positive and fruitful outcome if you follow your heart and allow your passion to guide you through the darker times.

I hope that readers will take a little something from this book and that it encourages thinking outside the box, as well as allowing readers to further their knowledge within the mysterious paranormal world.

"No man ever got very high by pulling other people down. The intelligent merchant does not knock his competitors. The sensible worker does not knock those who work with him. Don't knock your friends. Don't knock your enemies. Don't knock yourself"

Alfred Tennyson

Chapter 1

The Humming Lady of Aby

2015 was certainly a very interesting year, as it produced something of an obscure and rare opportunity to investigate a potential claim of a supposedly intriguing haunting.

In respect of the individuals of who were involved with the case, I have named the owners of the property as Mr and Mrs B to ensure that their identities remain a secret from the media and other individuals. I must also stress that the couple later moved on several months after me visiting the property.

Located in the East Lindsey district of Lincolnshire, lies a small village close to Alford. Named Aby, this tiny location was the setting for something that I still have no explanation for, and to this day the footage still makes me shudder with fear and confusion. The case was predominately undertaken by a group from Louth, but my former colleague and I were asked to join them after they alleged to have witnessed a plethora of different types of paranormal activity within the house.

Mr and Mrs B resided in an old cottage alongside their children and long serving dog in the heart of Aby, Lincolnshire. The initial meeting was purely to discuss the family's accounts of frightening ordeals, and I must admit the family and their experiences regularly enter my mind on a daily basis.

The family stated that they were regularly experiencing household objects disappearing and reappearing in several rooms, much to their annoyance and confusion. Sounds and smells were said to have materialised without explanation and the children reported that they regularly witnessed a lady in the upstairs playroom and on the landing area adjacent to that area. In my experience private cases require careful consideration and due caution because of their sensitivity as well as possible dangerous scenarios that can occur when dealing with a family with children residing at the address. However, they can be conducted correctly and with the correct ethical parameters, it will ensure that the greatest possible safety of everyone can be possibly accomplished.

I was not aware of the number of visits conducted at the family home by the Louth group prior to the investigation (my Colleague and I visited a few times prior to this to gather information) and I wasn't satisfied from the data I collected that there was sufficient information to require further investigation.

But when moving forward, how long should an investigation last for? Days, months, years? A question I've pondered many times across the years and have never been able to come to a suitable conclusion in relation to an individual investigation.

However, if you have a specific amount of time investigating at a particular location and have collated enough data and intel to satisfy your needs, then I suppose you have achieved your personal goals and aims in relation to what you deem as a complete investigation.

The family were very charming and came across as a no nonsense group of individuals who would stick together through anything. The visit on the day of the final investigation proved to be very fruitful and would lead us to something that I and others could not logically explain. On this occasion I believe the children were visiting the seaside, leaving Mr and Mrs B and their dog alone at the property.

The information shown below is extracted from notes taken by my Colleague and I, relating to the footage recorded at the property on the day of the visit.

Now I am one for data and measurements, as there is only so much you can do with witness testimonies and statements (although this is an extremely important and vital part of any investigation). I love to try and find possible trends and correlations in order to gauge any sort of common paths in hauntings, which led to me discovering what I call "The ghostly scenario" (of which we will cover in another chapter). Temperature is something I enjoy monitoring and I am aware that this has been closely investigated across the centuries within avenues of psychical research. It seems that temperature is quite a common trait in hauntings from around the globe and one cannot ignore its significance and underlining importance when sharp changes occurs.

On the day of the investigation several cameras were strategically placed around the property (with the agreement of Mr and Mrs B) and were left to record from our arrival continuing through late into the evening. The family were advised to conduct themselves as they would do on any standard day and with that Mr B swiftly left the property to carry on with his wood cutting activities.

The other group members were then left with Mrs B in the kitchen- located below the playroom upstairs. General conversation continued and plenty of cups of tea were consumed. I set up and positioned further cameras and temperature loggers, placed in accordance to where the family had reported experiencing the different types of phenomena.

The last camera set up was within the children's playroom itself. The room was a typical playroom where you would expect to see children in the midst of playtime and laughter, with many different types of toys strewn across the room. I remember the window being located on the left hand side of the far wall but nothing else of great importance that I had noted down on the day. The camera was set up on a tripod that captured a complete viewing angle from the far wall towards the door itself. The majority of the room was visible and clear upon reviewing, with no other possible access into the room itself aside from the door in full view of the lens.

The doors were of particular interest to me as I love to try to envisage a specific snapshot in time and the wonder that comes with it. Because the cottage was of a period construction and had all the original heavy wooden doors, to me it radiated a significant aurora in each of the rooms throughout the cottage.

As noted earlier, the final camera was placed in the children's playroom with the door firmly closed on departure of the room (you can view me exit the room from the footage recorded).

The day itself was a very long one (and I don't think I've ever consumed so much tea and coffee in all my life!) but I felt that it was a constructive day and I considered that the family were becoming a bit more relaxed in the fact that someone out there believed what they were reporting.

We left the property very late in the evening and the long drive back to Sleaford commenced, arriving home in the early hours of the morning. Following on from a very precarious sleep, I commenced what was to be a mammoth task of reviewing endless hours of footage, audio recordings and temperature points. To this day, I still have footage that has never been viewed and I often wonder whether anything else was caught on the cameras placed throughout the cottage.

Following a very frustrating start to the viewing, later on that afternoon I managed view the recordings of the children's playroom, which consumed six to seven hours' worth of footage taken on the day. Nine minutes and seven seconds into the footage is a time that I will always remember. At this particular moment I had managed to capture a type of phenomena that had been previously highlighted by Mr and Mrs B during the preliminary enquiries. I was alone in the office with my headphones firmly secured in place and pen and paper at the ready for anything to present itself on screen.

The camera reached the eight minute point and to my annoyance I could hear Mr B in the garden using his wood cutter in the distance. The house itself was very quiet but you can still hear the group members very faintly and Mrs B nattering away about her day. From my notes of the chronology of the day it seemed at this time myself and my colleague were in the dining room (adjacent to the kitchen) and we could clearly see everybody in the house accountable and present, with Mr B continuing to cut up wood in the garden.

At the nine minute mark, a very clear loud bang came through my headphones startling me. I referred to my notes to eradicate the noise and potential causes, did anyone close an internal door or maybe a cupboard door? The bang seemed to resonate from the children's playroom. The camera did not pick up anything that would appear strange to the observer, but my eyes were transfixed on the door within the room for some reason. Now at nine minutes, seven seconds, I began to quiver upon hearing what I can only be described as something straight out of a horror film.

I immediately removed the headphones due to being in utter shock and amazement.

I rewound the footage back to the same point, to replay what I had heard. Maybe I had imagined it? Maybe there was someone with me in the office? But I clarified that I was indeed alone, and continued replaying the audio that I believe would make anyone shudder.

At this moment I had caught (what appeared to be) a female humming within the children's playroom.

This humming sound lasts for approximately 6.2 seconds and the best way to describe the audio, is that of an older female humming a song or maybe a nursery rhyme. As stated earlier it struck me as part of a scene out of a horror film, and the camera did not pick up anyone within the room itself nor did the door open with someone entering the area. It was a complete mystery to me and very frightening to listen to through the headphones on the day of discovery.

It was somewhat funny in the same sense as I immediately called for my family to also take a listen and to clarify that I wasn't going mad! Family members who have listened to the audio have concurred my initial thoughts and I suppose gave me some clarification that I wasn't insane!!! The remainder of the footage failed to evidence anything of particular interest but again Mr B was clearly heard outside with the motions of cutting timbers of wood. The notes also clarified that no one else present in the property was upstairs at the time of the humming (and due to the clarity and crispness of the sound in relation to the camera's location) I am as certain as I can be that the audio is manifesting from within the children's playroom.

The chatter downstairs could not possibly have been heard that clearly from the point where the camera was located, and I also questioned why anyone from the group would be humming in such a manner in this particular scenario, and regarding the nature of this investigation? As for the toys present within the room, there was nothing noted that would have caused such a unique sound. Nor was there any such device to hold a recording and to unwittingly play a sound of this nature.

The temperature loggers did not produce any evidence of sub normal features throughout the house and the other cameras (of which not all have been reviewed) seemed to have picked up nothing else of any significance to the investigation.

So what did I capture in the children's playroom?

Although the investigation was set up fairly and monitored as thoroughly as we could possibly achieve, I still don't have a definitive answer in relation to what was recorded that day. The video camera itself was a Sony hard drive model, so initially no tapes or even compact disks were involved at the time of filming and everybody involved was accounted for. This piece of audio has yet to be explained and has been sent to many interested parties across the globe to see how they interpret the evidence captured from the village of Aby.

A few subsequent visits to Mr and Mrs B's home were conducted following the investigation, but according to the family the activity at the home had since begun to quieten.

As mentioned, I still have several more hours of footage from the downstairs hallway and dining room which still need to be reviewed.

The family continued to reside at the cottage for several months following on from the investigation, but I was later informed by Mr B that they had made the decision to move to pastures new. I believe when conducting a private case such as this, that it is paramount that the investigator aims to constantly reassure all individuals involved with the supposed haunting. Another important factor is to ensure that you explain and clarify normalities within the case, as this will most definitely put everyone involved at ease when conducting a methodical investigation.

The cottage in Aby will stay with me forever, and for many months after hearing the humming I did not sleep well. The family were fantastic throughout my interactions with them and I sincerely hope that they never experience similar events in their future.

To be quite frank, I wouldn't wish for anyone to experience the frightening types of phenomena that supposedly resided within the walls of the cottage in Aby.

"Nothing is too amazing to be true."

Michael Faraday

Chapter 2

"The Ghostly Scenario"

Why do people see ghosts? And more importantly what is a ghost?

There have been multiple accounts of supernatural manifestations for hundreds, if not thousands of years, but are we any closer to explaining and defining what a ghost is? The answer is unfortunately is no…

The apparition is surely the Holy Grail for any investigator or researcher, however considering accounts throughout time, we can clearly see that this is a very rare occurrence (predominately happening to someone who is not actually seeking ghosts). It's a long time frustration of mine, and something I've always pondered is whether or not there could be some defining factors that assist in witnessing an apparition. More importantly, we cannot ignore the human element that would most probably need to be there to assist with the occurrence, and to potentially be the catalyst for the manifestation to have the ability to unfold itself.

The word "ghost" is of an old English terminology translating as "to be aghast" (to be scared). This label is somewhat outdated and is quite vague in terms for what we maybe dealing with.

So, what is a "ghost"? Are we dealing with an energy source created by the human element? Or something residing within the environment anticipating that "trigger" moment (possibly the human mind) to kick start the initial manifestation enabling the presentation of itself to us?

The images depicting ghosts throughout time are indeed rather interesting, and the definition of the word itself has changed over periods of time also. The most commonly viewed images of a "ghost" is the typical white sheeted figure reminiscent of Scooby Doo characters, but this image originated hundreds of years ago along with the classic rattling chains to further increase the scare factor. Across time and reviewing reported past and present accounts, we know that most do not see those white sheeted figures with long rattling chains, but the accounts in fact describe seeing a human body of which most are fully clothed. (I must add at this stage I haven't noted any accounts of naked ghosts as of yet!).

What I also find very interesting is that most apparitions are also not reported as interacting with the lucky (or unlucky observer.)

This would therefore suggest that the apparition itself is likely to be unaware of the situation and could also be a possible time slip (the observer may not notice the change of environment, due to being transfixed on the apparition itself).

If we look at many published accounts, it is clear the majority of witnesses are never actually actively seeking ghosts, nor are they believers in the paranormal. But it should be noted that not all witness accounts are formally recorded or even discussed, as some are potentially too frightened to share their personal experiences.

So it's subsequently impossible to gauge any specific trend with regards to the two factors mentioned…

- Was the observer looking for ghosts?
- Were the observers believers in the paranormal?

As previously mentioned I work with data, trying to collate a sufficient amount and attempt to highlight any possible trends in relation to how and when people report seeing ghosts. This would then give us an indication as to areas of focus and (more importantly) gives an investigator a more probable chance of witnessing a ghost. Are we destined to know the factors relating to how manifestations occur? Maybe the universe is not ready to unlock its secrets at this stage of the human race's progression with life itself...

Within my methodology of investigating I have created what I have named "The ghostly scenario" constituting a series of important factors that must not be over looked or ignored when interviewing observers of apparitions. Accounts do vary of course, but with the below important questions they can present to us a trend in relation to re-occurring instances (subjects claiming to see the same apparition).

"The ghost factors"

We need to look at the following key fundamental areas, to try and gauge any specific conditions or problematic circumstances in which the phenomena could or can take place.

- Weather conditions

- Gender of the observer/s

- Time of day

- Location settings

- Specific area of apparent phenomena

- Current state of mind

- Description of the apparition

- How many observers witnessed the occurrence?

- Were the observer/s believers in the paranormal?

All of the above should be assessed and placed within a categorisation process, allowing any correlations to be made.

Easier said than done- as we all know the paranormal can be sporadic and spontaneous causing headaches for any investigator/researcher. But saying that, consideration of the above factors should give the investigator key information, of which may (with a number of instances) present information on trends.

Predominately, cases of witnesses proclaiming to see ghosts, are not interested nor are they believers in the supernatural. I find this rather fascinating in itself, as many would suggest that those who go in search of ghosts could be predominately creating them from within their own imaginations, thus causing a self produced ghost.

In 1973, eight members of the Toronto Society for Psychical Research (TSPR) embarked on a fascinating experiment to determine whether the human mind is the main influence for the psychokinetic activity that resides within hauntings. One of the members created a fictional male named Philip who was an aristocratic Englishman living during Oliver Cromwell's era during the 17th century. Within the experiment itself, all eight members studied Philip and tried to visualize the character as best as they could, in order to embed the characteristic and image (of what the group had agreed on) of Philip.

The group members met relentlessly across the period of a year, having drawn a picture of Philip inside the formed circle of the group. The sittings were not conducted in the dark, but done within different colour tones and also candle light. All of the members meditated within the sessions and then detailed what each of them had experienced during each meditation process.

As time went on, and with sessions becoming more productive, the group continued developing Philip into a familiar character that they could imagine and depict in detail. Rappings and table levitation occurred following a year of sessions, along with apparent communication with the imaginary ghost. It was conclusive enough for the TSPR to deem that the group had successfully created psychokinetic phenomenon without any sensitives or mediums in attendance.

A fine example of what the human mind can achieve, and so one does wonder whether the majority of experiences could indeed be summarised as self-created visualisations and settings, in order to supposedly witness an apparition. However, this does not account for *all* of the supposed witness testimonies, as there have been many publicised and well documented accounts of intelligent interactions with apparitions.

Certainly during my personal investigations into claims of hauntings, I have never witnessed anything remotely like an apparition, and my quest will continue in seeking the holy grail of ghost hunting. As mentioned previously I do often ponder the direction and significance of the quest to see an apparition for myself, but equally if I was to ever experience this, I would still aim to rationalise and further question what I had seen.

People have often told me that I am searching "too hard" and that I am therefore not "open" enough to witness the paranormal. This is another element that I have often considered in detail, and have questioned myself as to whether I am open minded enough to be receptive to the concept of ghosts.

There is no doubt in my mind that people experience ghostly phenomena, but what a ghost actually consists of is a completely separate debate. I feel that I am definitely open minded enough to have accepted that there are further mysteries yet to be discovered and solved. To say that I am closed minded would be a contradiction regarding my work within the paranormal, and also an easy get out clause as to why at this point I have never seen a ghost…

"We can definitely state that not all apparitions are spirits of the dead.

We cannot be certain that none of them are"

Guy Lyon Playfair

Chapter 3

"The Ruskington Horror"

The A15 is one of the major stretches of roads in England, running from Peterborough right up to Scawby, ending its run on the M180. This stretch of road shares stature with some of the most allegedly haunted roads in the UK. There have been a significant number of witness accounts reported including a plethora of different types of apparitions (of which on some occasions) have been utterly terrifying for the witnesses.

Within a particular area of the A15 located close to Sleaford Lincolnshire, a certain stretch of road has been on my radar for many years. I have lost count of the many claims from witnesses that experience one form or another of the supernatural at this particular location. The main type of occurrence that has been documented in witness interviews here, is that figures have been reportedly appearing in the road ahead of travelling vehicles. In some cases these figures appear to acknowledge that they are in the path of an oncoming vehicle by gesturing arms in the air as if to give the oncoming observer a forceful sign to slow down. Also duly noted, are accounts of disembodied body parts that seem to appear from within the moving vehicle and then swiftly move through the vehicle (and in some cases through the witness themselves) before swiftly exiting the other side.

Both experiences would be completely terrifying and could also contribute to a road traffic accident. What would you do if you came face to face with what resembled a human being stepping unexpectedly in front of your car, only for them to then completely disappear within seconds of the initial encounter? Freeze? Panic? Stop?

The majority of us wouldn't be able to fathom how we might react, but one thing is for certain, most people would surely stop to ascertain whether they had indeed collided with someone or something (frightening in itself). If you then slammed your brakes on and failed to hear any sound upon the anticipated impact, you would presumably find yourself franticly moving around the vehicle looking for dents, scratches or damage, although to your amazement and confusion everything appears to be intact. Therefore you can only conclude that you didn't actually hit anything… or did you?

As previously mentioned, ghosts are reported to have tendencies of being unaware of their surroundings, and are often witnessed conducting themselves as they would have within their physical lives.

At this point I would like to highlight the terminologies used i.e ghost and apparition, as they will both be frequently presented throughout the book as one entity; I view both terms as two blurred terminologies. Apparitions can and have been presented as animals and vehicles.

The terms "ghost" and "apparition" are both coined for certain types of phenomena, with audio being strongly linked to both and both also being linked to the haunting hypothesis. We can see that the two labels are somewhat generalised and causes confusion for giving definitive meanings as to what they depict. Let's face it, we know that there is no scientific evidence as to what these two terms actually mean. Labels within the paranormal have often been generated to assist us in processing an understanding and acceptance for the different types of claimed phenomena.

As we continue to discover more evidence, I believe these labels will evolve and this is beneficial to ensure adaptations are achieved in gaining a better overall understanding across all types of widely occurring phenomena.

One of the founders of The Society of Psychical Research Frederick Myers, wrote a publication called "Phantasms of the Dead" in which he debates ghosts and apparitions –

> *"Instead of describing a "ghost" as a dead person permitted to communicate with the living, let us define it as a manifestation of persistent personal energy- or as an indication that some kind of force is being exercised after death, which is in some way connected with a person previously known on earth."*

Studying research and witness testimonies that I have conducted over time, I have noted particular hot spots for supposed activity. This enabled me to concentrate on these specific areas and to follow up on whether anymore possible trends would present themselves, thus giving me a better possibility of maybe witnessing one of the types of phenomena regularly reported.

In one particular spot an occurrence took place back in 1997, which in fact caused huge media attention and worldwide cover of the story. I recall reading the story in my local newspaper with astonishment and questioning numerous aspects of the report at the time in my thoughts. The particular headline chosen by the media thoroughly amused me, as it was similar to that of a B movie horror title, which tickles me to this day.

You may only be enlightened to the humorous side of the hard hitting headline if you had visited the sleepy rural village of Ruskington. But in the true form of the media they dubbed the experience described by Mr Williams (pseudo name) as "The Ruskington Horror."

Who would have believed that twenty three years later I would find myself in my office with Mr Williams conducting a host of questions to armour my research into the alleged phenomena…? Was this synchronicity at play?

Mr William's account was certainly interesting and I will now present to you the reader the findings from the interview that day.

Upon finishing his shift at a nightclub in Lincoln, Mr Williams began making his way back to Sleaford in the early hours of the morning. He stated clearly early on during the interview, that he was not under the influence of any alcohol or drugs that could have affected his general state of mind or perception. Mr Williams reported that he took the same route to and from his place of employment each week, and didn't note of anything out of the ordinary occurring on any of his usual journeys (but unbeknownst to him at the time) this particular day was to change his life and also subsequently create a media storm.

Mr Williams approached a point on the road located close to another hotspot, named Temple Bruer Preceptory. I would also like to highlight here, that the incident did not occur in Ruskington as stated by the media, but in fact much further up the road and closer to Sleaford. The radio was playing at the time and Mr Williams was now not too far away from home. He recalls passing a house on the right hand side of the road when suddenly further on in the distance he saw what he described as a green illuminated bag coming towards the vehicle. (The appearance of the illuminated green colour was described as being similar to that of an illuminated watch)

Another aspect noted by Mr Williams was that the illuminated object included (what appeared to him as) an inner light coming from inside of the object itself. Driving a vehicle on a dark stretch of road, I would imagine it would have been difficult to make out at such a distance ahead of him, but unfazed Mr Williams continued travelling towards the illumination. His eyes transfixed on the object, he began to slow the vehicle down as he approached the illumination. The vehicle was now poised to now hit the illuminated object and at this point a prominent face appeared on the dashboard inside of the car.

Witnessing a face appear within the vehicle, Mr Williams described a feeling of sheer horror running through him, and throughout the interview he re-iterated several times that he was absolutely petrified. Due to him having slammed on the brakes, the vehicle skidded for a short period and then abruptly came to a halt.

Mr Williams was able to provide exquisite detail in relation to the face he saw and specifically noted the sharpness and clarity of the expression much to his horror. Mr Williams stated that the he considered the face to be that of a Greek male with olive toned skin.

Along with the face, a body developed and Mr Williams witnessed the male raise his arm up towards him, we can only assume that the apparition was possibly trying to interact with him or even warn Mr Williams of a possible danger. He continued describing the male's face with such clarity and the detail given regarding the appearance of apparition was phenomenal…Mr Williams even noted that he could see the pores in the skin of this male. Following the face appearing on the dashboard, the apparition continued through the vehicle, and disappeared without a trace or even a single sound to accompany what Mr Williams had seen.

The incident only lasted a matter of seconds but it caused Mr Williams to believe he had struck someone, although during his panic he began to rationalise and acknowledged that any impact would have created some sound. No bangs, no noise from the windscreen smashing… absolutely no sound occurred.

In his confused state and in the mist of the utter chaos occurring in the vehicle, Mr Williams attempted to turn the radio off and began to process what the hell had just happened to him. Staying close by the vehicle, he slowly and uneasily did a full 360 degree check to look for damage to the car, but no trace of anything was found. After confirming that the road ahead remained clear Mr Williams then began to drive away from the spot and continued his journey home. One can only imagine the sheer state he was left in, and also his struggle to contemplate what had just happened to him. Why him? Why that location?

One aspect I always consider when engaging with observers that have experienced apparent phenomena, is whether or not the observer has an interest in the paranormal or has close links to someone who may be. Mr Williams confirmed to me very clearly, that he had no interest at all in the paranormal. He admitted that that he didn't really believe in "ghosts", and was highly sceptical of all types of paranormal phenomena. Mr Williams arrived at his home in a frantic state and leapt straight out of the vehicle leaving the door and windows open. Running into the house he remembered slamming the front door and swiftly locking it behind him.

He then ran up the stairs and went straight into his bedroom where his wife was fast asleep. Still very much in shock, he then began to shout alarmingly about the series of events that had occurred, leaving a very confused and concerned Wife who was still half asleep after being awoken by Mr Williams' frantic shouting. Following a sleepless night Mr Williams was still unable to understand or even begin to try and place normality into what had happened in the early hours of the morning, and even talking about the event 23 years later still unnerved him somewhat.

So what was it that Mr Williams had witnessed? We can only contemplate and throw possible suggestions of what he encountered but one cannot deny that something had occurred. We were not there at the time and it would be very narrow minded to overlook the information and detailed account that he had provided.

I have carried out significant research into the area itself and the hot spots of alleged phenomena are all in close proximity of one another. Also, I note that there is a Ley line which runs to a point at Temple Bruer (located 0.1 miles from Mr Williams' incident).

I believe Temple Bruer is a possible contribution to the cause of these types of occurrences happening on the A15, and this is duly because of what lies at the end of temple Bruer road itself. If you travel down the very narrow road of which joins the A15, you do get a strange sense of something in the surrounding area. Now whether this is psychosomatic or whether I have genuinely felt something (for the first time ever) it's difficult to ignore the feeling you get when you travel down this road.

During my research, I have also learnt that there was once a medieval path that formerly crossed through the road, the latter is still in use today. The left hand side of the current road once housed a medieval village (smallholdings and enclosures). Towards the end of the road on the right hand side stands a beautiful Preceptory, it is one of the last remaining structures connected to the infamous Knights Templar. So what is left of the Preceptory today? Well only one of the towers remains but it still is fascinating inside, with many Masonic symbols and indications of mystery and wonder.

I have visited the tower many times and you always feel like you are being watched, or even examined by something- it's a very surreal place. As mentioned previously, there are supposed Ley lines that cross through the tower and many people have had strange experiences inside and outside of the location.

I have discovered that there have been two archaeological digs on the grounds itself with the first not so well documented, but according to Dr. G. Oliver (a Vicar from Scopwick, and also an amateur Archaeologist) he undertook a dig back in 1832 and proclaimed to have discovered some sinister and mysteries findings. He apparently unearthed supposed evidence of live burials, evidence of sacrificed infants, and subterranean vaults that were littered with burnt human remains that ran for miles towards a village called Wellingore. The second known dig was conducted by Sir William Henry St John Hope in 1907, he reported no evidence of underground vaults, but did discover two stairways descending to an underground Crypt. Evidence shows that the Knights Templar had acquired the majority of the land in the area of the acclaimed hotspots of activity, and it is known that at the Preceptory grounds, they would practice battle engagements and jousting.

The Knights Templar were an infamous and mysterious organisation, and one doesn't need to imagine too deeply to what other practices they once carried out within the Preceptory itself. Maybe the dark arts were performed, as they were renowned for their fascination with energies and the occult.

So based on the facts relating to this particular area (and it being frequently used by the Knights Templar) along with other cases being linked with this mysterious organisation, is it surprising people are experiencing strange phenomena? Mr Williams and several others have had frightening encounters in and around the Preceptory, and I am adamant that the Preceptory or grounds are in no doubt connected in some way to these experiences. It's very easy for people to rubbish personal claims of hauntings but one thing is for sure, I do believe that people are genuinely experiencing sub normal happenings.

If you do find yourself on a trip to Temple Bruer Preceptory, let's hope you don't have a frightening encounter like Mr Williams did, and that you don't bump into a ghostly knight within the eerie walls of the Preceptory- as that would be very unfortunate...

Of course, unless you are on the search for the phantoms that actively walk the surrounding area, then I am sure you would have found your own holy grail of truth...

"The soul is not shut up in the body like a bird cage. It radiates in all directions, and manifests itself outside the body as a light radiates from a glass globe"

Allan Kardec

Chapter 4

Ghosts, UFOS and the Almighty Lord

During recent research across the globe, it has been discovered that people who are not religious, are more likely to believe in and support others' beliefs in ghosts and UFOS. In today's society we are witnessing changes in beliefs and more importantly questioning of main stream religions, which has ultimately taken us in search of new avenues and theories to try and help us answer the problematic questions that we face in life.

Believing in something is extremely important for us all, we need this to enable us to feel that we have a meaning and purpose within life itself. Is this why those who are not religious, turn towards the supernatural hypothesis to supply their own conquest and stature in life? Our interests in the supernatural have been documented in writings as early as the first century A.D. One of which came from a Roman soldier named Pliny, who also wrote the world's very first encyclopaedia (it contained more than a million words and stretched to 37 volumes of work).

So we can accept that our interest with the supernatural has been with us for a very long time, and Pliny's literature on the ghost that haunted his realm, possibly gifted us the old stereotypical imagery that we are all very familiar with, of which is depicted in the view of a groaning rattling chained ghost.

Ancient humans reportedly used mythology as a way to try and understand what was happening in the world, and allowed us to have purpose to undergo the amazing journey of life itself.

> *"The primary function of myth is to move beyond the surface and penetrate our inmost core, laying bare our human nature. Mankind cannot part ways with myth.*
> *He can distance himself from organised religion, but not spirituality and myth."*

Extract taken from Benjamin Riggs' publication "Finding God in the Body".

UFOs are not publicised greatly back in the ancient realm but were otherwise accounted for as being mythological or supernatural beings. Ancient alien theorists believe that early imagery found around the world depicts unusual flying objects and beings of which are portrayed to be God like figures. Could it be possible that aliens were once on planet Earth and helped our civilisation onto a steady path of further enlightenment? If this was the case and an unusual alien civilisation did visit earth, then one could imagine that early humans may have immediately entered the religious path whilst trying to comprehend what they had been experiencing.

So we *could* establish a possible link between ancient Gods from another world, although not in the form of human beings, but of another species of minds, that have a much more developed mind set for the workings and understandings of the universe. This could also give credence to why we may have been visited over such a sustained period of time, and would give reasoning for regular check-ups on humanity (possibly querying why things in our current civilisation are going so drastically wrong). These ancient depictions of visitors from the skies could be the initial visits from these universal Gods. Is this how early human civilisation had such incredible knowledge regarding the stars, and interlinking the star system with ancient architecture that to this day, seems an incredible human effort and mathematical success?

We have established that human civilisations have recorded and possibly accounted supernatural forces of which are still being experienced to this day. But are UFOS and ghosts linked? The interdimensional hypothesis I find extremely fascinating in its own right, as this could surely be a huge link to both types of phenomena, and could also give us a general understanding of the two separate entities.

Many observers who claim to have seen a UFO or experience apparent abductions (soon after) begin to witness phenomena linked to the haunting hypothesis. Could these two separate phenomena be linked in anyway? I would suggest that it *is* possible, and if we take the interdimensional hypothesis, then one can be open to the fact that supernatural energies could be using the same gateways as elementals arriving from galaxies far far away. UFOs have often taken form in what looks like an energy plasma and could also be interlinked with ghostly apparitions. I cannot ignore the fact that these two different types of strange occurrences may be more closely associated than one could ever imagine.

Is ghost hunting the new spiritualist movement causing exceptional levels of intrigue from people around the world? Are we shunning main stream religion in place of personal conquests with the hope of establishing if there is indeed life after death? I truly feel that in the years to come we may see the rise of another alternative religion. This would be very appealing to the modern day person who has a definitive passion and connection to the paranormal realm.

From a personal perception towards UFO phenomenon and hauntings, I believe that the two different entities are linked in some way, and may be intertwined by the fact that both appear and possibly travel through periods of time itself.

There is no getting away from the fact that people can be susceptible to witnessing a UFO, and certainly a lot of people around the world witness apparitions. But the question is, how are these entities achieving this sub normal feat of visitation and duly presenting themselves to the unsuspecting observer? Are we ready to accept the fact that we are not alone? And also to peruse scientific proof of apparitions that reside and wander the lonely halls, castles and homes around the world? It's undoubtedly only a matter of time before we gain that vital piece of evidence that will lead us onto the correct path of fulfilment and enlightenment. Are we at the penultimate stage in the evolution of the human race, willing and ready to conceive that there is much more than meets the eye?

We must not ignore the possibility that ghosts/apparitions only present themselves when engaged by the living human observer, causing an interaction of energies. Some ghost/apparitions do seem to have a level of intelligence and could therefore sway towards using communication through telepathy of the observers' minds.

The question relating to whether we are "ready" is an interesting one, and although we are advancing in our technological dependency, we are losing the balance of spiritual well-being and overall care of the human mind. It also poses the consideration of whether early human beings were much more susceptible of witnessing strange types of phenomena, and I am purely basing this on the evidence of having very little distraction around to affect how the human mind worked. In modern day times, we truly do have a blinkered view, and I ponder whether the demise of witness accounts will dwindle as time goes by.

This however would surely not apply to the UFO phenomena therefore we may soon witness great evidential achievements of what UFOs are, due to technological advances in order to aid, support and understand such things by undertaking a higher intellectual level of thinking.

So we have established that we are all in search of one thing or another, whether it is that you believe in the almighty Lord, or that you believe in ghosts and UFOS. It is human nature to have that sense of belonging on the planet and more importantly that burning desire to uncover the secrets of what you believe and theorise about on a daily basis. I am not religious in anyway, nor am I a firm believer in ghosts or UFOs, but one thing is for certain;

there is an abundance of new things to uncover on Earth and within our galaxy, which we simply cannot comprehend at this moment in time.

There is no doubt whatsoever that observers do witness UFOs and ghosts. There are far too many credible accounts for each sector of the paranormal, to simply discount and ignore. But the real question is- what are the two types of phenomena and what are the mechanics within the sources?

Will we ever find the answer that may lead us to unlocking the mysteries within our galaxies? Because I truly hope that one day, we obtain that spiritual enlightenment and furthermore expand our knowledge and understanding of the universe.

It could even give us a more complete understating of one another, and maybe give the human race a well need slap around the face. We are by no means kind to one another, and it does beg the question, why would anyone visit a planet that is on the path of self-destruction, leading only to a possible extinction for human kind.

"Mythology is not a lie, mythology is poetry, it is metaphorical. It has been well said that mythology is the penultimate truth–penultimate because the ultimate cannot be put into words. It is beyond words. Beyond images, beyond that bounding rim of the Buddhist Wheel of Becoming. Mythology pitches the mind beyond that rim, to what can be known but not told."

Joseph Campbell

Inside the Bull I' Th' Thorn Inn

"Looking for ghosts" at the infamous Golden Fleece in York, England

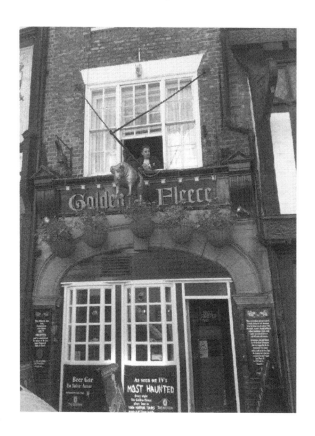

"Alone and forgotten" - Haverholme Priory, Ewerby, Lincolnshire, England

Stonebow and Guildhall Lincoln, England

Supposed phantom horse and carriage sounds are heard over the bridge at Haverholme, Lincolnshire, England

Haunting Temple Bruer Preceptory, Lincolnshire, England

Over the bridge to Haverholme Priory, Lincs, England

Chapter 5

Paranormal Wars

I wonder if anyone else out there feels the same as me, and questions whether the paranormal world has indeed become a vast no man's land of arguing, backbiting and general unkindness to each other. What I refer to specifically in this chapter is some ghost hunting groups, events companies, paranormal teams and fame hungry individuals. Predominantly those who are waiting in the trenches for their holy grail of evidence to propel at others in order to embed their status as supposed paranormal Gods. I have witnessed first-hand, how some groups treat other groups on a regular basis; it's like a war out in the field! Why, and how has it become like this?

There are a number of groups out there who are continuously posting their contuned regular proclaimed hard hitting evidence and this in affect gives permission for the paranormal world to comment, judge, and simply to rip apart and purposefully throw back into that groups unsuspecting faces. Although in the minority- there are a coalition of smaller groups and individual researchers and investigators out there that are willing to help each other out. These teams will happily engage with one another and amalgamate for investigations, discuss findings, and willingly demonstrate their methods to one another without judgement. This I must add, is the only conceivable way forward, to continue our research within the paranormal, and to gain any sort of forward movement in to securing clearer fundamental ideologies.

Overall, the vast majority of teams seem to snipe and viciously tear apart claims of evidence or findings displayed for public viewing by other groups. Are these jealous actions?

Some comments are constructive observations from others which is to be expected- as one must remember that when publicising any sort of apparent evidential phenomena, you will always receive some level of scepticism. Although in my view, most are trying to climb the imaginary paranormal ladder of fame, by belittling the supposed evidence gathered, and providing their self-proclaimed more knowledgeable input, with no reasoning (and more importantly) no respect paid to the individual or team. I for one, am extremely concerned by all this unnecessary commotion created in the realm of the ghost hunting arena. It feels as though we are all steadily losing sight of what we set out to achieve. There are numerous groups that simply crave the paranormal "celebrity status" gained by participants of some well-known entertainment programmes. I believe it to be these individuals and TV programmes that served as a catalyst for the behaviour of some investigators and groups today.

Social media has had a monumental influence within our everyday lives and also pretty much every sector and avenue you can think of. The internet has certainly changed the fundamental manner in which we think, create, communicate and more importantly the way we treat each other. The ghost hunting world has seen itself evolve due to the use of the internet and has attributed many different aspects to the utilisation of information that is presented and exchanged. I have engaged in multiple conversations regarding how the social media aspect has presented itself as a double edged sword to the paranormal community.

Time prior to the internet provided us very limited sources of information. I can remember cutting out newspaper articles about local hauntings and also (more to the point) people participated in discussions and debates regarding the relevant topic on a one to one basis more frequently than we witness now. Word of mouth was also the only real way of making people aware that you were involved in aspects of the paranormal and awareness would never have reached the dizzy heights of which social media so easily achieves today. The Library and other literature obtained were really the only sources that you could extract information from, and I must admit, this is a much more desired approach for me personally when I conduct any sort of investigation.

What has the internet achieved for the paranormal realm then? Well we can certainly agree that it has increased the interest of the general public, and has given many people who cannot attend ghost hunts or investigations, access into live videos at supposed haunted locations. This to me, is a huge benefit of social media and the internet in general. There are far more people interested nowadays in the subjects being portrayed, than there were back in the early 90s, so you could summarise that the paranormal has nudged further into the reaches of people across the globe. Not only that, but it's incredible to consider that groups/teams and individuals can share more information than ever before…surely another huge positive here for the internet and the paranormal…..

But...

What the internet (and in particular social media) has done is created this pedestal of supposed fame.

Send those virtual stars and groups/individuals receive money. Share the feeds and personal/group pages and popularity grows among adoring fans and followers. A particular red flag for me is when you notice groups continuously ask people to share the live feeds and to "send those stars". For me, this throws doubt over the intentions of those acting in such a way, and I think a few groups/individuals need to re-assess the aims of which they had originally set out to achieve. Finding evidence and sharing ideologies should be the ethos at the core of each and every group, individual and live feed enthusiast.

It does make me curious into what investigators like the late Harry Price would extract from all these arguments and confrontations, or moreover his thoughts to the internet's alternative effect on the paranormal community in general. I can only imagine he may be somewhat bemused, disgusted and alarmed at the amount of hatred and the sheer numbers of uncooperative and closed minded individuals we have. Above all, we all share the same passion and the same end goal in sight don't we?

Why is it not possible that we all work together as we progress further into the field in the hope of bringing the attention of today's scientists to the paranormal umbrella?

On a positive note, it should be duly recognised that there are individuals and groups that are pushing forward with some amazing work and research within the field. It's these individuals that I truly admire and can only aspire that greater numbers will come to appreciate the work they are currently undertaking. Unfortunately though, the astounding work that has is currently being conducted, is somewhat overshadowed by the general idiocy presented by these fame hungry individuals.

Is it because of the childish behaviour within the majority of paranormal groups that some academics of the science world inadvertently side step the paranormal, and do not consider it to be serious enough for them to do any sort of credible research on? Maybe it's time to try and come together; this may bring new techniques, new thinking and in turn a much more constructive understanding within in the paranormal. Yes the big profitable, entertainment based, ghost companies will still exist, but we should remember that they are not attempting to gather any sort of evidence that can be presented in an academic sense or for a greater purpose. The majority are only interested in the financial gain this brings to them. It would be a long-time dream of mine if all groups were more tolerant of each other and respectful, and maybe we could all start to comprise some sort of database where evidence could be stored and analysed inclusively. Just an idea, but think of the possibilities we could all achieve if we started to work as one…

The large venues will be overlooked for once (and research in additional areas that could gift us all the answers to which most yearn) may be a big possibility with cohesive working practices. Will this dream come true? I fear that sadly it won't, and in reality the future is bleak if we cannot wake up to the fact that the hostilities and the battles of teams aiming to get the upper hand will continue, thus creating a ripple effect for credible research. Ultimately meaning that all of the good intentions and progress made will be crushed, and I for one don't want this to happen. Do you?

The Paranormal is an expansive cluster of topics, subjects and questions (with even more puzzling answers) derived from brave investigators, parapsychologists and scientists who dare to publicly state their own theory or logical explanations for things that science struggles to explain, inviting the world to respond with their own personal opinions.

I have been looking for answers for more than twenty one years and have built a vast library of data from researching and investigating throughout the years. I currently spend most of my time investigating ghosts, poltergeists and apparitions. Following every book that I read or every investigation carried out there is one definitive question that is always in the back of my mind and slaps me in the face from time to time- will the paranormal ever be proved or disproved once and for all?

Is the paranormal something that can, or is intended to be unlocked?

How would we all respond to ground breaking evidence of the afterlife?

What would it mean for us to discover life on another planet?

These are just an example of some common questions that would arise and of course would have huge implications on humanity. Some however, may argue that we already know the answers and do not need to seek out anymore clarification of the unknown.

Others simply have a thirst for that golden opportunity to hold a piece of flabbergasting evidence, that they will use to springboard their ego to celebrity stature and immortality of paranormal legends. Others would simply long for an answer their own personal questions.

No matter who we are or what we do in life, we all desire the same answers in one form or another, but as I have asked, is it feasible that it can proved or disproved?

My personal opinion is, not yet....

I truly believe as humans inhabiting this tiny blue planet in space, that we are simply not ready for answers that could truly change the way we think and act towards humanity as a whole. The reasoning behind this conclusion is that if we consider the subject of ghosts and poltergeists, it is an age old topic that spans over a sustained period of time.

Many have tried to understand and explain in rational terms how an outbreak of poltergeist activity occurs, but again people either accept or shoot a theory down in flames causing some forward thinkers to go back to the drawing board. The technology (or simply the lack of it) could have been an important factor relating to the evidence gathered but with our current technological advances we have no excuses on that side of things.

At present, the mass numbers of smart phones, digital cameras, camcorders and other technology owned and used on our planet is colossal. Furthermore it is reasonable for us to have expected a proportionate percentage of ghostly sightings of the white lady, or that somebody experiencing poltergeist activity must have recorded that chair moving of its own accord. Although in reality, what we are left with is hoaxers clogging up the field in their quest for financial gain. Some say that this was the cause of "The Cock Lane Ghost" back in 1762, or simply fraudsters that hunger the publics' attention. The field is crammed with confusion and is therefore continually frustrating for those serious enough to try to understand and study the paranormal. Are these ghosts camera shy because they have the answer to humanity? The jury is still out on that particular subject, and the world watches on, waiting with bated breath.

We do however learn of rare cases that do truly defy explanation, and on occasion view footage or images that lean towards something supernatural being in force. Have these snippets of the unexplained knowingly permitted us to view and record them through forces unknown, in a bid to merely dangle the carrot in front of us mortal humans to further entice and keep us on the path of the truth? This may be so, and has genuinely gripped my attention for a long time and I'm sure will continue to do so for many years to come.

The paranormal field has sadly become more reminiscent of a circus in recent times, but then having said that, has it not always been that way? I conclude that we all need to work together towards the same goal in one form or another, it is essential that we share and encourage ideas and theories, and discourage radiating any sort of negativity (as it is completely demoralising and damaging) causing some to wash their hands of the paranormal, and more frequently give up their paranormal aspirations completely.

It could just be the case that one of you out there has the key to share and unlock the mysteries that encompass the paranormal; you might well just be sitting on something incredible. If we collaborate and head in the same direction, it may be the case that we can gather increased amounts of evidence, have a more complex understanding of the paranormal, and have the potential to unlock that defining moment in humanity.

Clearly the answers are out there, but we should all endeavour to promote (not just to the supernatural) that we are fully prepared for the truth- but to prove to ourselves that the human race can show level headedness, compassion and has the ability to step forward as one. In essence, we are all the same, no matter which walk of life you are from. And of course you never know, you may become the main cause of a new rare case of ghostly occurrences where you view the reflection of yourself in an alternative dimension; looking through from the other side, to a dimension you once walked and breathed in...

As your ghostly footsteps pitter-patter down to your once dearly loved spot, would you allow a group of investigators and scientists to record you? Or would you lucidly shy away, leaving them to continue speculating as to the origin of those footsteps and the sound that manifested in the presence of the eagerly anticipated investigators?

"For a hundred years a few scientists, rather half-heartedly, have been trying to find out these things – without success. Even the 'spirit hypothesis' does not cover the 'appearance' of a psychic coach-and-pair! These are things that we do not understand, and science, to its eternal shame, is making little attempt to understand them."

Harry Price

Chapter 6

<u>Spirited Pubs and Inns</u>

I must admit that I have embarked on somewhat of a personal love affair and general affinity for supposed haunted pubs and inns over the years. I mean what could be better than being sat inside a 13th century coaching inn on a dark winter's evening, with the roar of the open fire and the flickering glow of the dancing flames lighting up the interior of the surroundings? It's a setting many of us have experienced, and goes hand in hand with that atmospheric if not idyllic setting for a ghost story or two. I have been extremely lucky throughout my period of intrigue with ghosts and hauntings, and have visited numerous supposed haunted pubs and inns within England's ancient Isle. Anyone who shares my interest in ghosts will likely be aware of, or have visited a pub or inn with its own portfolio of ghost stories and experiences attached to the building and in some cases surrounding areas.

Whilst writing this book I wanted to include a section on haunted pubs, but I soon realised that I could probably write several publications on the specific topic itself, as once you start to peel back the imagery and fascination with these buildings, you find yourself with many different aspects and ideologies for how and why, we have so many acclaimed haunted pubs and inns.

I will begin this chapter with possibly the very first allegedly haunted pub that I visited, located in the stunning surroundings of the rolling hills of the Derbyshire landscape. The Bull i'th'Thorn Inn (shut its doors in November 2017) is a typical English ancient inn, with period interiors of wooden panelling, hand crafted seating attire and bold beautiful English oak stained striking beams throughout the whole of the property.

My first visit to the property was born on the back of whispers that the inn was branded as one of "the most haunted places in Derbyshire," and of course the title certainly sparks interest with anyone who has a curiosity for ghosts and phantoms. I was lucky enough to visit the Inn several times prior to completing the initial interview with the Landlord at that time, who was certainly a jovial chap and some would say slightly eccentric in the way he paraded himself around the building. I personally took to him very quickly, and he wasn't shy in telling us about the stories and witnesses that claimed to have experienced paranormal phenomenon at the location. I recall the day extremely well as it certainly triggered my intense enthusiasm with haunted public houses, and also it was a day where the Landlord had closed the doors to the public (a demise in traffic at the inn caused the landlord to shut its doors several times during the working week). The day time slot allowed me a substantial amount of time with the Landlord, and more importantly to observe the natural noises and movements of this stunning property.

The inn started its life as a farmhouse and it dates back as far as around seven hundred years. It is situated on the remote part of an old Roman road between Chester and Buxton, both of which locations, have many historic ties. The building itself first became a hostelry in 1472 and was aptly named "The Bull", and one can imagine the interesting plethora of characters and clientele that once set foot in the ancient inn to quench their thirsts from their weary travels throughout the seasons in the Derbyshire countryside.

The Landlord began to inform me of several different accounts of strange happenings that predominately started when he took over the pub. He would passionately explain how on occasions he would hear his name being called out, however at the time he was the sole resident at the inn. This type of phenomena is quite common, but if we delve into the sceptical side of things, then you will discover that medical hearing issues like Tinnitus can lure the brain into thinking that you are hearing a sound and quite often in the sense that the person in question can hear their own name being called. Now I am not by any means disregarding anybody's experience of strange audio phenomena. But you must retain a balanced and calculated mind set when investigating claims of hauntings (something I have worked on and gained over the years of investigating). Other sound references were discussed too, one of which was witnessed by several diners at the time of the incident, which further gripped my attention.

It was a bright spring day and the inn had a scattering of tables filled with people enjoying their Sunday dinners and divulging in light conversation (an ambience experienced at most restaurants and country inns). As the afternoon progressed several diners began departed and gave their thanks to the Landlord for his hospitality, when all of a sudden, close to the far side of the wooden panelled wall a child sobbing could be heard. The Landlord did state that he and several other diners heard the sombre sound of what seemed to be a young girl crying.

The specific times and length of the sound were not accounted for and so we can only depict what the Landlord decided to share with us, but something I have always been attuned with is recognising when a person is genuine. The Landlord told this story with great intent and of course for him to have chosen to share an experience like this with me is my privilege. Respect is paramount when investigating the paranormal, and lack of this has continued rearing its ugly head in recent times. People's experiences are their own very personal moments which they entrust you with- to listen. In some cases you must exercise caution dependent upon the situation, as belief plays a huge part in people's lives and your comments (if not chosen correctly) can cause damage to the person's well-being and mind set.

The exuberant Landlord followed with another fascinating experience which was felt by a number of people within the inn. Regular temperature fluctuations were felt throughout the property and as we know, this type of phenomena goes hand in hand with hauntings.

My investigations are predominately centred on temperature readings, as it is a factor that can account for credible scientific data if conducted and recorded correctly. I have several temperature related apparatus that I use on every investigation, as I believe that this type of phenomena is a common occurrence when discussing and researching historic haunting cases.

It seemed that the Landlord had certainly experienced several unaccountable types of phenomenon, but the story that really captured me, was the explanation of the Roman ghost. Situated behind the inn was a large open field (part of which was adjoined to the inn itself) and at the time was being used as campsite for visitors to pitch up and enjoy the local landscape. The Landlord detailed an occasion where a couple who were staying at the campsite, had seen what they described as a Roman soldier dressed in battle attire, march across the open field. Possibly the biggest ambition for any ghost hunter is to witness such an event, and not only that but the apparition of a Roman soldier. Upon finishing the Roman soldier story, I immediately began to think of young Harry Martindale and his brush with the legion of Roman ghosts travelling through the cellar walls of the Treasurers house in York.

Did the couple indeed witness the apparition or was it a trick of the light? The mind is an intrinsically complex organ and can cause us to believe that we are seeing and hearing things that are not always there. Nevertheless, we cannot discount every experience as possible mind tricks… there are far too many accounts that question everything we know about science. Let's face the facts...

- The human race is continuingly changing its path and perception in life.
- Science and historic facts are forever being rewritten and evolving in time.

From my first visit to an apparent haunted inn, I began to anticipate the possibilities as to why such a large number of inns and pubs are associated with hauntings? Something I still speculate over today is why and how so many of these places are apparently haunted.

Why are these building such strong magnets for ghosts and their witness' accounts?

I have been approached by multiple establishments over the years to visit and investigate their claims of reported hauntings, but one must be cautious when accepting such offers. I have witnessed that the majority of these instances simply turn out to be self-advertising, money orientated motives of the proprietors.

Eighty one miles north from the inn is the historic city of York, which compromises of ancient pubs, inns, snickleways, and awe inspiring reminders of centuries gone by. The city has been a huge catalyst for me to further my research over the years as it is home to a huge concentration of ghost stories that range from Roman soldiers to former disgruntled Landlords that are not yet ready to relinquish control over the property they once resided in.

The first time I visited the city, it immediately captivated my true being and I feel that because the city is bursting with so much history certain layers in time can contribute (if not be instrumental) to what we call paranormal activity. The city certainly isn't shy, with its blasé approach of projecting out its deep rooted ghost stories, which I think only assists the mysticism of the location.

What struck me about this city is that the locals are extremely proud of their prevailing history and more importantly, the ghost stories that reside and pulsate within the ancient city walls. Locals are more than happy to discuss and present their own personal accounts of strange happenings that have occurred in local premises such as shops and bars. Another staple conversation to be had whilst in York is recommendations of how many pubs and inns are located within the city walls. I have been reliably informed by locals that there are (supposedly) 365 pubs and Inns contained within the city! That's a lot of pubs!

And most certainly a higher chance of possible ghost sightings within the many diverse, and colourful pasts that these buildings have witnessed.

The Shambles by night doesn't leave anything to the imagination; as you are suddenly transported back in time and it really does infuse you with the surroundings and atmosphere of times gone by. You can certainly pick up on the echoes of the past as you walk down the tiny, bumpy cobbled street. You can almost hear the bustling noise of the locals and the smell of fresh live animal kills hung from the underside of each building.

At the end of The Shambles you will come face to face with a legendary little place that has been somewhat of a tourist attraction for many years now.

The Golden Fleece inn, and has to be one of the most infamous pubs in the UK. So infamous in fact, that tourists from around the world flock to the building. It's a place I have often visited and I have also stayed for the weekend. It ticks all the boxes for that Olde English inn, with its narrow features and wonky floors, it really does have that nostalgic emotive feel and history emanates throughout the building.

The building itself dates back to at least the 16th century and has had its fair share of historic moments and characters inhabiting it across time. The ghost stories sewn into the fabric of the building, range from the apparition of Lady Peckett (Wife of John Peckett who was Mayor of York around 1702 and also owned the Golden Fleece within this time period) to a former Landlord who allegedly hung himself behind the bar still used at the inn today. I have spent a good deal of time at the inn and have visited for overnight stays as well as flying visits, across different times of the day and evening, and I am yet to experience anything out of the ordinary.

However, as an investigator I find it imperative to interview witnesses of proclaimed occurrences. The staff at the inn have experienced very unusual happenings, and they are present to of a much more amount of time at the property compared to any ghost hunter would wish to dream of. I think it's relevant that we duly note that a large sustained time spent at any property would more than likely increase the possibility of coming face to face with what we label as a ghost. As I mentioned earlier, the Fleece is very well known for its history and ghosts, with realisation that they could be possibly be:

"The most haunted pub in York".

However this label of being "The Most Haunted" has been used frequently over time for countless locations and buildings entwined with ghost stories.

Harry Price once famously labelled one of his publications regarding his investigation of Borley Rectory, "The Most Haunted House in England".

This, I think you will agree, is an extremely bold statement to say the least. What gives a place, the right to label itself as "The Most Haunted"?

Does it calculate the total amount of experiences? Or is it the volume of sightings per square foot? Nobody really knows, and in my opinion I would presume generally boils down to marketing.

If we take the cities of York and Derby as a head to head on ghost stories, we have two places that believe and state that they are the "The Most Haunted City in England," and compete on a daily basis with their world celebrated ghost tours and events that draw investigators and tourists alike. Both have extensive history, and could well be what they proclaim, as we are aware that the layers of time cause a channel of events which could lend a hand towards ghostly phenomenon, but is this enough for them to be labelled, "The Most Haunted?" for me- this isn't enough.

More recently the quiet village of Pluckley, in England has been given the title of being, "The Most Haunted Village in England," and superseding that, they also hold the Guinness world record for this sought after title. Will these self-awarded, coveted titles just spurn others on to try and outdo them and in order to claim similar labels?

The titles are self-appointed, and one must be careful when venturing out to spend time investigating claims of hauntings in this sort of setting.

The city of York is rightly very proud of its history and ghost stories, the tourism trade is a big deal but can bring with it opportunities that unfortunately are open to abuse. Businesses can really grasp on to this and use it in a negative or misleading manner for their own financial gain. I do not condone this. If anything, I think it's fantastic that locations such as pubs and inns can utilise their ghost stories to gain publicity and interest for the paranormal. This is beneficial for both parties but be warned... many self-publicised hauntings can, and have been conjured up out of nowhere to draw unsuspecting customers in. It certainly pays to research the place you wish to visit along with its stories, as well as talking to witnesses. This will ultimately aid your decision on whether more time spent there would be the appropriate action in relation to your desired investigation, or simply your search for the truth.

As noted early on, the UK has a vast amount of rumoured haunted pubs and inns, with a diverse amount of phenomenon that people claim to have experienced. In addition, historic archives also indicate that these locations have a lengthy history of ghostly goings on within the fabric of the buildings around the ancient Isle.

I have frequented high numbers of buildings and locations that have portrayed encapsulating ghost stories, but I've always been in awe of the places that are not keen on publicising the instances that have occurred. In some areas of the UK I have found that people remain closed minded regarding discussing or considering possibilities of hauntings and consider the subject a taboo one.

So why do we have so many apparent haunted inns and pubs here in the UK?

Well, I have detailed several key elements that could present definitive factors relating to the hauntings taking place, and also to determine the characteristics as to *why* so many people have paranormal experiences within certain these types of buildings:

- Many of these buildings have been prevalent throughout multiple periods of time and layers of our history.
- Most of these places frequently have a high concentration of people in situ at any given time.
- High levels of human emotional attachment to the location.
- Pubs and inns can attract a plenitude of different types of people.
- Concentration and filtration of human emotional engagement over lengthy periods of time.
- Family connections to the properties.
- Possible creation of harmonic energies (related to the above possible factor).
- Many cases of reported deaths connected to the properties.
- Contrasting religious beliefs throughout the life span of the location.

- Sixty thousand pubs and inns stand within the UK alone.

The above presented elements all have an underlining common component that I would estimate is prevalent in the majority of, if not all, ghostly visitations- that being the presence of the (living) human mind. But it does pose the question, as to whether or not ghosts are active when the human elements are not around.

"Does a ghost haunt a house when no one is at home?"

A thought provoking scenario that I have contemplated is that we can only assume that the human element must be in attendance, in order for the ghostly phenomenon to commence.

Another striking if not definitive factor from the previous list is the awareness and accepted level of high human emotion. These places have been rife with happiness and sadness throughout long periods of time, and one can imagine the emotional stamps that have been left in the buildings over this time. This could possibly be a part of that perfect ghostly phenomenon to present itself to the unsuspecting observer.

All houses wherein men have lived and died
are haunted houses. Through the open doors
the harmless phantoms on their errands glide
with feet that make no sound upon the floors.

Henry Wadsworth Longfellow

Chapter 7

Haverholme Priory

Four miles north east of my hometown Sleaford, is a mysterious place that I often visit, and have done since I was around eleven years old. The remaining ruins we see today, are a shadow of its past symbolism, power and former stature.

The monastery was predominately founded in 1137 and was handed over to the Cistercian monks of The Fountains Abbey. In 1139 the Cistercian order rejected the site and instead chose to reside at Louth Park Abbey. Haverholme was then offered to Gilbert of Sempringham and his Gilbertine order sent nuns and brothers from Sempringham to inhabit the priory and surrounding grounds, which at the time was undergoing developments to become the grand architectural design it later became known as.

The Gilbertines not only inherited the priory but the surrounding area that enclosed the stunning priory itself. They were responsible for maintaining the adjacent fens where local legend teased of hidden treasure that the monks supposedly stowed away in the period of Henry IIIV's reign in England. If this were to be true, I would imagine this was during Henry's dissolution of the priory itself.

Haverholme Priory has seen a fair amount of untold history and one can only envisage the secrets that it has entombed within its enduring and prevalent history. In 1539 after

Henry IIIV dissolved the order, the priory was purchased by the Finch-Hatton family, and was used as a family home for the century following this.

This stunning place remained in its prime until its fate was pronounced in 1920. The property was put up for general sale by the family and in 1926 the priory was sold to an American lady, with her ultimate desire and intention being to export the priory back to her home country. This project soon became reality and stone by stone, segment by segment, the priory was carefully deconstructed, loaded and transported to the docks of Liverpool for the long voyage towards America.

This I would of thought would have been an intricate web of planning and belief that the property would arrive all in one piece. It is recorded that the majority of the priory almost complete was waiting for the go ahead of embarking on its final journey and expectation of a new home, (I wonder what the monks of the Gilbertine order would have thought to the dismantling of this holy building). However the lady in question who so longed for the priory to be a part of her home country suddenly died in a train crash and of course never actually saw the priory resurrected in her home country. Coincidence? Or was something else at play to ensure that the priory didn't leave its home.

The ruins visible today are just a tower and a segment of the ornamental balustrade and are only what was left from this huge project of dismantling the building stone by stone for a journey that didn't quite make it. But what is left reminds us of what once was a magnificent and special place for its residence and a holy plethora of religious orders that resided within. As I have mentioned in previous chapters I believe that belief has an underlining affect on the human soul and character of a person. Belief in any sort of form is such a significant affect on the human mind and may be the key to why people witness ghosts of certain time periods in a specific setting.

I remember the very first time I rode my bike as youngster towards the ruins and even then has still left a mark on my passion and overall outlook on the paranormal. The priory has a perfect idyllic surrounding for nature and natural resource for the inhabitants that once resided within the building. Surrounded by flat fen land of which in adjacent to the location has a beautiful river that has a very thought provoking and atmospheric feel to the surrounding area.

Over the years especially in the early days of visitation to the location, I have compiled many stories that have been attained to the ruins and the surrounding fen land including the river of which still is prevalent to this day.

The main supposed occurrence that still to this day is reported is to be of an audible echoing sound of footsteps within the ruin themselves. I have spent Hours at this location and regular visits continue to this day for me as I feel a strong connection to the place and the surrounding grounds, but I am still in wait to hear such sounds residing within the ruins themselves.

In recent years I have found myself questioning why we take certain paths and choose certain decisions in life and especially those that would fall within the synchronicity hypothesis.

Maybe there is more of a reason for my connection to the site and not just of being a past visitor since the early years of interest in the paranormal.

Personally I have never experienced anything to the magnitude of anything of a sub normal nature but I am hopeful that I may get that rare opportunity of a strange occurrence or two within my lifetime as we all know these things are extremely spontaneous and of a rare nature. However I would not deem above mentioned occurrences enough for my clarification and reasoning for what may have occurred. As the years have rolled on I have become far more sceptical to claims of hauntings, but in the same time has also grown the interest to another level of understanding.

Are we ready to know the truth?

Places like Haverholme priory are an amazing setting for your mind to clear and to allow your sub conscious thoughts to arise and maybe this could be a factor to what people may or may not be experiencing. The majority of us will agree that the human mind is an incredible organ and possibly as we evolve we may find that we discover new parts of the brain that will allow us to become far more susceptible to our environment and also to feel certain energies that our past ancestors were so in tune with.

We cannot deny that the subconscious proportion of our brain may have a lot to answer for when dealing with ghostly claims. It's also a possibility that a section of the brain may be causing imprints of past information (during processing) to cause holographic visualisations of objects and living organisms. Still, to this day we don't have a plentiful supply of answers for causes of hauntings and ghosts, but only hypothetical theories where science cannot yet deny or confirm exactly what is happening to people.

There has been some encouraging progress from certain lifelong researchers with regards to infrasound which could provide a strong link to people's personal experiences in relation to what we label as hauntings. Although this cannot definitively link this to all experiences, and therefore it would not be viable to securely place the haunting hypothesis within this area of scientific study. It's refreshing to see a handful of researchers who are seeking the truth regarding what people claim to have experienced. It is almost impossible to re-create an environment of air tight control or lab type settings to monitor ghostly phenomenon... unless of course there is a university somewhere in the world that has its own resident ghost...

Innumerable locations are susceptible to natural occurrences thus giving investigators and researchers more to ponder regarding the large scope of "normal" explanations which serve to acquit the majority of claims about ghostly phenomena.

Haverholme Priory is most definitely a location which is susceptible to being thrashed by the elements, and has an abundance of Lincolnshire wildlife to add to the mix of its standard conditions. This also provides another point to be considered in possible cases of proclaimed activity.

Very close to the ruins of the priory is a beautiful piece of architecture that was built in 1893 where I have again spent various hours waiting patiently for any odd occurrence to happen. There have been multiple claims of unnatural occurrences prevalent throughout the years that I have been engaged in ghost sightings. I have observed through detailed observer accounts, claims and research, that increased amounts of supposed paranormal activity is linked to the bridge itself rather than the priory, which I find fascinating enthralling in itself.

In particular, certain claims depict a phantom horse and carriage- this been experienced by several people in the area. Hooded figures have also been supposedly witnessed travelling over the bridge appearing to move in the direction of the priory.

If you follow the river Slea from the bridge at Haverholme, you will stumble across an array of ancient trees and also in your eyeline to the left you will see the priory ruins arising from the distant horizon. There is no denying it's a breath-taking image when walking around the grounds during sunset. It really is an extraordinary site. Now, not only have people claimed to have had experiences on the bridge and priory but the river itself is purportedly a hub of activity also.

There are rife myths and legends bounded to the priory and to this day occurrences are still being widely conveyed.

But why haunt a priory?

Well, if we break it down and strip back every possible meaning and theory, we are left with the underwhelming feature of religion and more importantly belief.

Belief is a towering factor in evolution of human kind and we cannot discount this passion and more importantly the certainty for what we believe in. Are these ancient sites more prone to paranormal encounters? Or are people more attuned to the belief that ancient sites should be haunted?

Throughout this book I have championed the fact that maybe ancient sites are far more favourable to the ghost hypotheses, but we should not disregard the notion that the underlining fact may be that we are the ones that could possibly conjure up ghosts from within. I will never disregard (nor should any serious investigator) anyone's personal experience, as this would demonstrate pure narrow mindedness, and is unjustifiable. There are a myriad of accounts of paranormal activity across the globe, and I firmly believe that because of the substantial volume we cannot brush aside every account (but instead must consider each on its own merits) to do so would be an injustice to the informant.

A great deal of locations similar to Haverholme Priory are truly captivating to me due to their architecture. They bring bewilderment, enchantment and also bring the past back to life. Are these ancient places conduits for certain ghostly phenomena to take place? Effectively, we can continue to research and accumulate witness statements, but until you *visit* a specific location for its individuality, I would unquestionably challenge anybody's affirmative stance on disbelieving that strange occurrences happen at these historic sites.

It is said that the Spirits of buried men
oft come to this wicked world again;
that the churchyard turf is often trod,
by the unlaid tenants of tomb and sod.
That the midnight sea itself is swept
by those who have long beneath it slept.
And they say of this old, mossy wood
whose hoary trunks have for ages stood.
That every knoll and dim-lit glade

is haunted at night by its restless Shade.

Isaac McLellan

Chapter 8

The Erratic Nature of the Modern Day

Ghost Hunter

So, where did this affinity and admiration begin for our intrigue of paranormal notions that have been readily divulged throughout the centuries? I would certainly be strongly inclined to place the marker (as it were) upon humans' first learning of death, and the surrounding questionability of *why* death occurs and then more precisely whether there is an afterlife…

The curiosity of death has undeniably been present since the dawn of time, and the more that we discover, the more we yearn to have accelerated knowledge of how (and most importantly why) things occur within the universe.

I surmise that this forceful thirst for knowledge and understanding, will ultimately continue until the day arrives where our species will cease to exist, tumbling to our own fateful demise.

Albeit, let us be optimistic with regards to human kind, and the possibility of the ever increasing amounts of breaking scientific discoveries, that could lead us onto a path of correctness within the universal motions. There is already in this day and age, a strong indication that humans could colonise another planet… strong progressive thinking and moreover, empathy for one another (it seems to me) is the key to the survival of human race on this rock that we call earth.

If we break the barriers regarding acceptance- allowing each other to be at one with ourselves- and become receptive to new ideology and at peace with one another, that would in itself be a formidable mountain to have climbed.

Our affinity with death as previously noted, has been reported throughout time, but the breakthrough modern day spirituality movement that began its path in 1848 (predominately started by the Fox sisters, in Hydesville New York) would have marked the beginning of a new awakening and realisation of the possibility of life after death. Closer to the point, it pushed this ideology for spirit communication to the forefront of the general publics' domain, and you could inevitably imagine the excitement at the possibility of speaking to your departed loved ones. It was most definitely a lifeline of hope for many people worldwide, as we are all too aware, that death is a prominent reminder that each of us will one day depart this physical plane.

As the popularity of spirit communication spread like wild fire around the world in the 1800's, scientists and other academics began to look into compelling area, in order to observe and monitor such claims of subnormal happenings. Their united interests paved the way for (now renowned) rational thinking organisations such as the SPR (Society for Psychical Research) and The Ghost Club, formed to study and document claims of psychical notions.

The engrossment with the above mentioned groups unequivocally picked up pace over time. They accrued a magnitude of scholars, writers and prestigious supporters spanning the globe. They all shared the same passion and desire to try and unlock the answers to limitless questions that had arisen throughout the spiritualist movement and beyond in history.

Charles Dickens, Sir William Crookes, Sir Arthur Conan Doyle, Fredrick W.H.Myers, Sir William F.Barrett, all names that are celebrated in our history books for various achievements, and who all also linked through their intrigue and burning desire to search for the truth. The truth, being to discover what people were experiencing, whether it be a session at a séance in Paris, or to understand ESP (Extra Sensory Perception) they all had the profound interest in adopting it as their mission to try and understand the mystical mechanics of anomalous proclaimed phenomenon from around the globe.

Their works have evidently become instrumental catalytic forms of further enlightenment for any modern day ghost hunter or researcher of the unknown. Without doubt, I feel that organisations like the SPR have acted as welcome beacons to attract the more serious investigator into the paranormal, and from my perspective, their continued efforts today are setting the stage for innovation of understanding. Turning the clocks forward from the very early days of the ghost club and the SPR, a gentleman named Harry Price joined the SPR in 1920. His initial interests within the paranormal started at the tender age of fifteen linked to a reputably subnormal personal experience. Devoting his life's work to parapsychology, his work is still being studied to this day.

He was a strong and passionate figure but by comparison, someone who also relished the limelight. His continued self-publicity scattered Harry Price across various media streams through his work. This caused apparent upset within the SPR and soon Harry found himself scorned by certain individuals questioning why the publicity was needed.

Through Harry Price's extensive work within psychical research, in 1925 he established the NLPR (National Laboratory for Psychical Research) based principally in Queensberry Palace, London. It was used extensively to discover the truth about psychical claims that would witness proclaimed mediums from across the world, take part in experiments concocted by Harry Price in laboratory conditions (I often marvel over whether today's mediums would entertain any type of laboratory setting for a methodical approach into what powers they profess to have).

Harry Price's work was frankly awe-inspiring and he was positively a chap I would have aspired to meet, and have the opportunity to acquire a more comprehensive insight into his methodology, research, and involvement into those cases that had all the notions of apparent hauntings. Now, some may disagree with me here, but I sense that he was the creator of methodical investigating. What I am insinuating with this bold statement is of course, the personal approach he took when conducting various cases throughout his career, presenting such a charged sense of direction.

It is not necessary to probe too far into his considerable research to indicate how he conducted a methodical investigation. The Borley Rectory case remains to this day, one of the most prominent cases of all time. And not only distinguished for being esteemed as, "The Most Haunted House in England," but for my part, it was his perspective intuitive, and patient approach to the case.

The majority of visitors and investigators to the property at Borley Rectory were given instructions from Harry Price, consisting of detailed reports and his own thorough observations. These could be considered to be the very first guidance notes for investigators of spontaneous cases. Even today, modern day researchers follow a comparable path and process to that of Harry Price and the ways in which he conducted his thinking, and involvement with spontaneous hauntings.

So what did the future (at the time of Harry Price) hold for future researchers and investigators of psychical research?

Well it was unquestionably a promising outlook, as the SPR went from strength to strength regarding its involvement with certain individuals, and the progress of research at the time was categorically promising.

Springing forward fifty years in time to the 1990s, and organisations like the SPR were still thriving. With the mental acquisitiveness and fundamental appetite for answers in unlocking the mysterious questions that opened up new thinking towards strange phenomenon. In '90s England, there were a small number of groups and teams conducting meetings across the country, in their local pubs or village halls, to discuss their appreciation and enthusiasm relating to paranormal phenomenon. I have memories of seeing an advertisement in a local newspaper during this time that was specifically reaching out to people who had an interest into ghosts. I would strongly advocate that in the '90s ghosts were still an "off limits subject," and were almost considered comical, but that would seemingly undergo a transition into acceptance, and light being shone on the subject through television and of course the birth of the internet.

The simplicity of groups in the '90s was something to be admired, they held a harmonic, modest respect for each other, but also endeavoured to learn the truth for regarding what people consider as ghosts. Has this been lost in time? Losing that elementary reason as to why people originally set out to know the truth?

Love it or hate it, but television programs had a monumental impact on people's outlook, and more importantly hard hitting realisation, that people do have strange experiences of which are still not understood. You can most definitely argue the case that paranormal TV shows were stimulants for numerous researchers that remain involved in today's work. Nonetheless, as with many components in today's world, they can be of negative utilisation. Certainly for me watching "Ghostwatch," it had an immense impact on laying the foundations for what has (and continues to be) a search for the truth. Television without fail, impacted the paranormal, and it assuredly has had its pros and cons, but we must not forget that TV shows have brought that inquisitiveness and recognition of the subject to a much wider audience. It has propelled a new level of probing into the subject of ghosts and also created a certain level of captivation of the public's interest in the matter.

The public's curiosity regarding ghosts was most definitely on the increase thanks to film and TV shows. The general acceptance of the paranormal was on the rise, and I saw for myself the number of groups that also had the passion for the paranormal on a steady incline. However these numbers are small compared with ever increasing numbers that we see today. This was not solely down to TV, as there was a big helping hand from the birth of the internet. This new access to the information highway, exploded into everyday life and soon became a very monumental invention that has interchanged everyday life. I witnessed the setups of local groups around the country radically change in a particularly short period of time in my life. The internet was an unsparing tool that became contemptuous, not simply for the paranormal but in everyday life. As demonstrated, everything can be utilised into whatever positive or negative notion the individual desires to imply.

I vividly remember the birth of the internet and even now reminiscing, I could never have contemplated how this ground breaking invention would change the paranormal community overnight. The public's demand and enjoyment really catapulted its notion and came to rely on it as a tool to research and understand all aspects of ghosts. The popularity of public ghosts hunts boomed, and the success of ghost hunting companies increased tenfold in the early 2000s. Personally at the time I was beyond excited, I was eagerly anticipating the fact that people's perception of ghosts was going to change for the better.

The debate will continue until the end of time, as to whether the internet overall was a positive motion for the paranormal, but I will argue my point that I feel it has created certain investigators, whose involvement has stemmed from completely misplaced intentions.

Back in the '90s there were no live feed investigations, nor was there any disrespect towards others who shared a common interest. Respect was prevailing in the early days and everyone who had the same devotion and interest, monumentally shared compassion towards others alike.

The appeal has and will continue to bring together different types of people who all share that *same* key initial intrigue. To my mind there are certainly many out there who have created a smoke screen of greed and dissolution of the subject matter. There are still large numbers of serious investigators and researchers in today's field to understand ghosts, but the ever increasing erratic nature of new paranormal hosts continues to fester, drawing us backwards and in the completely wrong direction for springing this subject matter into a more seriously considered topic.

From the creation of the internet, and also the increasing involvement of paranormal TV shows, I have been a spectator to the introduction of multiple takes on individual methods, practices, and attitudes to investigating.

"The Armchair Investigator"

Due to the ever increasing choice of paranormal TV shows and social media platforms, the public can easily have self-filmed investigations projected straight onto their screens and devices, without ever leaving their favourite armchair. This (albeit it amazingly wonderful) can also lead to presumptions and stereotypes being created for how the public assume all investigators conduct themselves within an investigative environment. As standard, you should cast a wide net as to whether running around with a night vision camera displaying the incorrect date, is a balanced or methodical approach to investigating claims of hauntings. The armchair investigator is an expert in how they perceive other investigators should project themselves, and are unable (or unwilling) to accept or comprehend any opinion that differs to their own in relation to the ethics of paranormal investigating.

"The Lazy Ghost Hunter"

A new, special breed of investigator has been unearthed. Characterised by the common trait that they have endured very limited time, have minimal experience, and moreover, a lack of involvement with investigating claims of hauntings. The lazy investigator will be comfortable with disregarding people's experiences (more worryingly) with no serious understanding, and without having amassed sufficient collective evidence of occurrences. The lazy ghost hunter has only their own personal interests at heart. The internet has proved to be a monumental success, and provides a convenient access point for the lazy ghost hunter- It's all too easy to repeatedly type into search engines, perusing and gathering content that they deem an ample amount of credible information to put towards a case.

"The Internet Live Investigator"

Rapidly on the increase, we see this intriguing, relatively new concept to so-called investigating. This type of investigator (not all) plays their role out on screen, pleading for constant gratitude and with their slogan always present (that all important part of the feed) ***"Please please please like my page and share"*** The internet has a lot to answer for with regards to this new variety of investigators, streaming live in every group, page and channel. This investigator predominately profits from their own personal ego trip, and ardently waits to announce that they have reached towards their audience count. It has undoubtedly induced the growth of numberless communities hanging on their every word, but this cannot be constructive to people's perception on paranormal investigating... can it? Individuals like these luxuriate on the level of emotional output that the audience transfer when sending over those virtual stars. In my eyes, it's likely that the majority of these live feed investigators did kick off with the initial intensions of searching for the truth, but have been ensnared in with that dangling carrot of opportunity, and pedestal of fame and fortune. I do not completely absolve the live feed investigator, as there are some of whom take a more serious approach to investigating and this I applaud. The live feeds also convey that allure of the paranormal into people's lives, who may not be able to attend public events, conventions or other events, and can nourish their personal intrigue for a very positive notion. Nonetheless, critically the majority do not think in an ethical way and are lost in that moment of imaginary self-imposed fame, given to them by their online fan clubs.

"The Thrill Seeker"

Spurred on by the public's increasing mesmerisation with the paranormal, this brought forth the popularisation of public ghosts hunts across the country. I was that thrill seeking individual at one time, and thrived on the excitement and possibility of maybe coming face to face with a ghost. Public events (if conducted well) can be a fruitful approach to people's general interest in the topic. But they can also portray examples of how not to conduct yourself in an investigative environment. For my part, experiences of public ghost hunts have enabled me to witness the good, the bad, and the downright ugly. My first involvement in the public ghost arena, was what I would consider as my initial awakening to the volume of groups and companies that were conducting events throughout the year. One thing that is prevalent within the bulk of these events is the individuals who enjoy that scare factor.

They have watched the films and TV shows portraying the entertaining side of it all. These people flourish from those emotionally gripping hands on event that compares to starring in your own supernatural blockbuster with you playing the leading role. These are not investigators but nerveless, they still share the same pursuit as everyone else, albeit from a narrow angle of the paranormal. The thrill seeker is a regular attendee to public events and will hand pick locations for that unmitigated scare factor.

For me, the internet will continue to create these new directions for people who are interested in the paranormal, but it's how you present yourself, and also your definitive purpose, that will render you into one of notions of the modern day ghost hunter.

The ongoing work and continued progress made thus far by serious researchers and investigators, is extensively overlooked. Most are far more interested in streaming individuals prancing around the woods after dark. People seem to find this more entertaining than reading journals and papers on critical research into hauntings. I consider myself very lucky to have experienced several avenues within the paranormal field. These range from having been involved in public events, running my own group, and now focusing on researching and investigating as a lone individual. It has definitely calibrated my way of thinking and led me to be more inclined to adopt a more serious determination surrounding what I am seeking.

Not only has my philosophy changed, but I have also found myself conducting investigations using a more methodical approach than previously. I too am guilty of being influenced by TV shows (as media has a cosmic effect on our daily lives) but throughout my experiences and inclusion searching for ghosts, I have apprised a more acute intention of looking for the truth.

The work of certain individuals from the SPR (Society for Psychical Research) has evidenced a mammoth impact on how I approach the paranormal completely. Whereas prior to this, my investigation methods were fundamentally guided by TV shows, this has since undoubtedly moved closer towards a more scientific effort in investigating claims of hauntings.

The paramount aspect that I have learnt throughout the years, is that ethical aspects *must* be considered prior to commencing any sort of investigation. Witness interviews have positively been a key strand for me, and I have learnt that this is predominately the initial starting point (as it were) for conducting any investigation. My methods have also propelled forward with tangible measurements that one can assess and surmise on certain claims of hauntings. Within my own work, my main focus at this time encircles temperature within hauntings. Temperature has historically been linked to hauntings and is something that we are able to accurately measure.

I am still studying new methods and wish to methodically conduct more composite investigations, into claims of hauntings. My nature has certainly changed over time, and I am positive that we haven't yet seen all of the different possible species of the modern ghost hunter.

It is your personal choice and direction of purpose that will mould you into the investigator that you aim to be, whatever the nature of the outcome you want to achieve, but remember this…..

Most of those who are interested in the paranormal, share the same motivating force behind the questions they emit.

Are we not all trying to seek the same truth?

A footstep, a low throbbing in the walls, a noise of falling weights that never fell. Weird whispers, bells that rang without hand, door handles turn'd when none was at the door. And bolted doors that open'd of themselves.

Alfred Tennyson

Chapter 9

<u>Seeking the Truth</u>

My continuous journey into seeking the truth has undoubtedly caused me to question my beliefs and reasoning surrounding why people claim to see ghosts. There has been vast comprehensive work conducted by certain individuals who aspire to progress the subject matter, in order to allow us to scientifically understand what people are experiencing. From my own personal research, I am certain beyond reasonable doubt, that some observers genuinely experience hauntings and witness ghosts. Unfortunately, I think that further scientific research can most definitely be undertaken, but that it has a weakened case to manage due to the entertainment aspect of ghost hunting and everything this entails. I do sense that one day there will be breakthrough findings with regards to what people are experiencing, and I hope that individuals' perceptions of ghosts will rightly gravitate away from the Scooby doo motions.

Critical and methodical thinking should be paramount for any serious investigator. The majority of those looking for ghosts are far too easily caught up in the moment of excitement, fuelling a misconception of what may or may not be occurring. Let us not forget that realisation of your inner belief. Your mind can play tricks on you and also cause short-sightedness in assessing the reality of a situation.

The majority will permit their beliefs to fundamentally present or manifest an occurrence which subsequently fits their personal brief on how they wish for that instance to turn out.

In my opinion, a number of investigators have lost their purpose and have over time neglected the main reason to why they initially started their own personal journey into unknown forces. Is it time we should re-asses how we approach the haunting hypothesis? I have witnessed many investigators who are now revaluating their methods and considering more scientific based studies towards ghosts. Let's be honest... flash emitting LED lights are not really telling us anything significant and wouldn't present any definitive evidence towards ghostly apparitions.

It also imperative to consider and assess, the many different types of natural phenomenon that could give substantial reasoning as to why some individuals claim to see ghosts. Frequency could be a possible reasoning for people witnessing what they believe to be a ghost. The human ear can only hear a certain range of frequencies and is unable to hear frequencies of below 20 Hertz (Hz). However, that isn't to say that that the human body as a whole is unable to detect low or high frequencies, as it has been reported that a certain range of frequencies can cause hallucinations (a frequency of 18.9 Hz) In our modern day world, we rely so much on technology, most of which can emit certain frequencies. It is scientifically proven that environmental changes can also emit certain frequencies along with earthquakes, volcanoes and other climatic changes.

We also have adequate evidence to illustrate that some witnesses may have experienced a chemical interaction leading to feelings of dread and hallucinations. This can occur from various types of mould prevalent in old properties, castles and premises, and may indicate why so many apparent repeat occurrences take place in particular locations.

The geology is also an area of importance to be explored. This could present reasoning as to why certain places are supposedly haunted and have had extensive witness testimonies. Could the land itself be another key factor and provide further clues? It would be a very compelling report to calculate the geology of these sites, and maybe to give an inclination for favourable factors to present themselves.

We must explore all the possible natural motions that could link to the *real* reason as to why people see ghosts.

However, we must not be in denial that all proclaimed occurrences are caused from natural phenomenon. There are some very unique and tantalising historic cases that would insinuate that unknown forces are at play and that there is something that we do not yet fully understand. I hope that my ongoing research will present me with proportionate material, allowing me to continue to evaluate my own theories and understating towards the ghostly hypothesis.

Do not believe everything you encounter…

Challenge everything that occurs within your investigations…

Be true to yourself and others…

At this current stage within my research I have by no means conclusive evidence to suggest what ghosts are, but I am certain that collectively, we may one day attain the truth. Are we as a species ready to accept the truth?

Would we be able to accept the reality of the possibility of an afterlife?

I hope you have enjoyed reading my first
publication on seeking the truth.

I wish you well on your personal journey to
explore, discover and above all learn the truth.

ACKNOWLEDGEMENTS

Firstly, I believe that I should thank you the reader for purchasing my very first publication. The journey has been extremely interesting to say the least, and I am still endeavouring to discover the truth on ghosts. I hope that you take at least one thing away from my writing and that it causes you to ponder ever more about the strange and mystifying topic of the supernatural.

I would like to thank Mark Steadman for his monumental influence on my paranormal journey. Things happen for a reason and I do not believe that his gift came to me by accident. The book he gave me still resides on my bookshelf and will forever be a key factor in my journey for seeking the truth.

My wife Gemma has been immensely understanding throughout my journey and involvement in the paranormal. The lost time together is something that I cannot retrieve, but I am eternally thankful for her continued patience and support.

Appendix:

Below are a number of further recommended publications that have had a profound effect on my curiosity into the unknown and may be of interest to you the reader –

1. *Hauntings and Apparitions* – Andrew Mackenzie - Published on behalf of The Society for Psychical Research.

2. *Human Personality and Its Survival of Bodily Death* – Frederic W. H. Myers – First published in 1903

3. *The Unknown Power* – Guy Lyon Playfair – Published 1977 - Guy Lyon Playfair.

4. *The Haunted Pub Guide* - Guy Lyon Playfair – Published 1985

5. *In Search of Ghosts* – Hans Holzer – Published 1980

6. *Restless Realm* – Barry.R.Frankish – Published 2020

7. *The Paranormal* – Stan Gooch – Published 1978

8. *Guidance Notes for Investigators of Spontaneous Cases* – Steven T.Parsons - Published 2018.

9. *The Reality of The Paranormal* – Arthur Ellison – Published 1988 – A comprehensive scientific exploration of the supernatural.

10. *The Scole Experiment – Scientific Evidence for Life After Death* – Grant & Jane Solomon – Published 1999.

11. *In Search of Ancient Mysteries* – Alan and Sally Landsburg – Published 1975.

12. *Mystery of the Ancients – Early spacemen & the Mayas* – Eric and Craig Umland – Published 1975.

13. *Alien Contact – The first fifty years* – Jenny Randles – Published 1997.

14. *The Poltergeist Phenomenon – An Investigation into Psychic Disturbances* – John and Anne Spencer – Published 1996.

15. *Other Worlds – Space, Superspace and the Quantum Universe* – Paul Davies – Published 1982.

16. *Superminds – An Enquiry into the Paranormal* – Professor John Taylor – Published 1975.

17. *Explaining the Unexplained – Mysteries of the Paranormal* – Hans J.Eysenck and Carl Sargent – Published 1982.

18. *The Flying Cow* – Guy Playfair – Published 1975.

19. *Life After Life* – Raymond Moody JR – Published 1975.

20. *Paganism and the Occult – A Manifesto for Christian Action* – Kevin Logan – Published 1988.

21. *Ouija – The Most Dangerous Game* – Stoker Hunt – Published 1985.

22. *The Cylces of Heaven – Cosmic Forces and what They are Doing to You* – Guy L Playfair and Scott Hill – Published 1978.

23. *The Cock Lane Ghost – Murder, Sex & Haunting in Dr Johnson's London* – Paul Chambers – Published 2006.

24. *The Poltergeist Prince of London – The Remarkable True Story of the Battersea Poltergeist* – Shirley Hitchings & James Clark- Published 2013.

25. *New Evidences in Psychical Research* – J.Arthur Hill – Published 1911.

26. *Ghosts of the Broads* – Chas.Sampson – Published 1973.

27. *The South Shields Poltergeist* – Michael J.Hallowell & Daniel W.Ritson – Published 2008

28. *Riddle of the Future – A modern Study of Precognition* – Andrew Mackenzie – Published 1974.

29. *Poltergeist – Tales of the Supernatural* – Harry Price – Published 1945.

30. *Mediumship and Survival – A Century of Investigations* – Alan Gauld – Published 1983.

31. *Fifty Years of Psychical Research* – Harry. Price – Published 1939.

Facebook page
www.facebook.com/paranormalseekeroftruth

Instagram - @tom.warrington.pure_paranormal

Printed in Great Britain
by Amazon